CW00518300

EASY MUSSELS COOKBOOK

50 DELICIOUS MUSSEL RECIPES

By
BookSumo Press
Copyright © by Saxonberg Associates
All rights reserved

Published by
BookSumo Press, a DBA of Saxonberg Associates
http://www.booksumo.com/

About the Author.

BookSumo Press is a publisher of unique, easy, and healthy cookbooks.

Our cookbooks span all topics and all subjects. If you want a deep dive into the possibilities of cooking with any type of ingredient. Then BookSumo Press is your go to place for robust yet simple and delicious cookbooks and recipes. Whether you are looking for great tasting pressure cooker recipes or authentic ethic and cultural food. BookSumo Press has a delicious and easy cookbook for you.

With simple ingredients, and even simpler step-by-step instructions BookSumo cookbooks get everyone in the kitchen chefing delicious meals.

BookSumo is an independent publisher of books operating in the beautiful Garden State (NJ) and our team of chefs and kitchen experts are here to teach, eat, and be merry!

INTRODUCTION

Welcome to *The Effortless Chef Series*! Thank you for taking the time to purchase this cookbook.

Come take a journey into the delights of easy cooking. The point of this cookbook and all BookSumo Press cookbooks is to exemplify the effortless nature of cooking simply.

In this book we focus on cooking Mussels. You will find that even though the recipes are simple, the taste of the dishes are quite amazing.

So will you take an adventure in simple cooking? If the answer is yes please consult the table of contents to find the dishes you are most interested in.

Once you are ready, jump right in and start cooking.

— BookSumo Press

TABLE OF CONTENTS

Any Issues? Contact Us

If you find that something important to you is missing from this book please contact us at info@booksumo.com.

We will take your concerns into consideration when the 2nd edition of this book is published. And we will keep you updated!

— BookSumo Press

LEGAL NOTES

ALL RIGHTS RESERVED. NO PART OF THIS BOOK MAY BE REPRODUCED OR TRANSMITTED IN ANY FORM OR BY ANY MEANS. PHOTOCOPYING, POSTING ONLINE, AND / OR DIGITAL COPYING IS STRICTLY PROHIBITED UNLESS WRITTEN PERMISSION IS GRANTED BY THE BOOK'S PUBLISHING COMPANY. LIMITED USE OF THE BOOK'S TEXT IS PERMITTED FOR USE IN REVIEWS WRITTEN FOR THE PUBLIC.

COMMON ABBREVIATIONS

cup(s)	C.
tablespoon	tbsp
teaspoon	tsp
ounce	oz.
pound	lb

*All units used are standard American measurements

CHAPTER 1: EASY MUSSELS RECIPES

SIMPLE MUSSEL PLATTER

Ingredients

- 3/4 C. white wine
- 3/4 C. tomato and clam juice cocktail
- 3 cloves garlic - peeled and sliced
- 1/2 tsp crushed red pepper flakes
- 1 lb. mussels, cleaned and debearded
- 3 tbsp butter

Directions

- In a soup pan, mix together the juice cocktail, wine, garlic and red pepper flakes and bring to a boil. Stir in the mussels and boil, covered for about 4-6 minutes. Remove the mussels which are not opened.
- Transfer the mussels in a large bowl and cover with a foil paper to keep them warm. Remove the cooking liquid, reserving 1 C. of the liquid with the garlic in the pan. Cook the liquid till it reduces to 3/4 of the C.
- Add the butter and stir till melted completely.
- Serve the mussels with the sauce.

Servings per Recipe: 3

Timing Information:

Preparation	10 m
Cooking	10 m
Total Time	20 m

Nutritional Information:

Calories	214 kcal
Fat	12 g
Carbohydrates	10.5g
Protein	5.3 g
Cholesterol	42 mg
Sodium	371 mg

* Percent Daily Values are based on a 2,000 calorie diet.

LIGHT SUMMER MUSSELS

Ingredients

- 1 tbsp butter
- 1 tbsp olive oil
- 2 tbsp minced garlic
- 2 tbsp minced shallots
- 1 tbsp capers
- 3 C. canned tomato sauce
- 1 tbsp Italian seasoning
- 1/2 tsp red pepper flakes
- 1 lb. mussels, cleaned and debearded
- 1 C. chopped green onions

Directions

- In a skillet, heat the oil and butter on medium heat and sauté the shallots, garlic and capers for about 5 minutes.
- Stir in the Italian herbs, tomato sauce and red pepper flakes and reduce the heat to medium-low.
- Simmer, covered for about 10 minutes.
- Stir in the mussels and increase the heat to medium-high.
- Cook, covered for about 10 minutes.
- Discard any unopened mussels from the skillet.
- Serve with a garnishing of the green onions.

Servings per Recipe: 4

Timing Information:

Preparation	20 m
Cooking	25 m
Total Time	45 m

Nutritional Information:

Calories	142 kcal
Fat	7.1 g
Carbohydrates	15.8g
Protein	6.9 g
Cholesterol	17 mg
Sodium	1102 mg

* Percent Daily Values are based on a 2,000 calorie diet.

VENETIAN MUSSELS

Ingredients

- 4 quarts mussels, cleaned and debearded
- 2 cloves garlic, minced
- 1 onion, chopped
- 6 tbsp chopped fresh parsley
- 1 bay leaf
- 1/4 tsp dried thyme
- 2 C. white wine
- 3 tbsp butter, divided

Directions

- In a large pan, add the wine, onion, garlic, 1/4 C. of the parsley, thyme, bay leaf and 2 tbsp of the butter and bring to a boil.
- Reduce the heat and simmer for about 2 minutes.
- Stir in the mussels and cook, covered for about 3-4 minutes.
- Transfer the mussels in a bowl and cover with a foil paper to keep them warm.
- Strain the cooking liquid and place in the pan with the remaining butter and parsley.
- Cook the liquid till the butter is melted completely.
- Serve the mussels with the sauce.

Servings per Recipe: 4

Timing Information:

Preparation	35 m
Cooking	15 m
Total Time	50 m

Nutritional Information:

Calories	298 kcal
Fat	10.1 g
Carbohydrates	10.3g
Protein	18.6 g
Cholesterol	70 mg
Sodium	330 mg

* Percent Daily Values are based on a 2,000 calorie diet.

NAPA VALLEY SPICY BASIL MUSSELS

Ingredients

- 2 tbsp butter
- 3 tbsp minced garlic
- 4 shallots, chopped
- 4 C. beef broth
- 1 jalapeno pepper, minced
- 1 red chili pepper, minced
- 4 fresh tomatoes, coarsely chopped
- 20 fresh basil leaves, torn
- 2 C. white wine
- 1 tbsp cornstarch
- 1/2 C. light cream
- 5 lb. fresh mussels, scrubbed and debearded

Directions

- In a large soup pan, melt the butter on medium heat and sauté the shallots and garlic till browned lightly.
- Add the red chile pepper, jalapeño and a splash of the broth and simmer for a few minutes.
- Stir in the remaining broth, white wine, tomatoes and basil and bring to a boil. Meanwhile in a bowl, mix together the cornstarch and a little amount of the light cream.
- In the pan, add the remaining light cream and cornstarch mixture and bring to a boil. Cook for about 5 minutes.

Servings per Recipe: 4

Timing Information:

Preparation	20 m
Cooking	20 m
Total Time	40 m

Nutritional Information:

Calories	413 kcal
Fat	13.8 g
Carbohydrates	27.2g
Protein	24 g
Cholesterol	80 mg
Sodium	1109 mg

* Percent Daily Values are based on a 2,000 calorie diet.

MIAMI MUSSEL VINAIGRETTE

Ingredients

- 24 fresh mussels, scrubbed and debearded
- 1 small green bell pepper, seeded and diced
- 1 small red bell pepper, seeded and diced
- 1 small yellow bell peppers, seeded and diced
- 1/2 C. olive oil
- 1/4 C. red wine vinegar
- 2 tbsp chopped fresh parsley
- 1 hard-cooked egg, chopped
- 1/2 tsp salt
- 1 pinch ground black pepper

Directions

- In a large pan, add 1-inch of the water and bring to a boil.
- Add the mussels and cook, covered for about 3-5 minutes, then drain well.
- Discard any unopened mussels.
- Remove one side of each shells and place in a large serving plate.
- In a bowl, add the remaining ingredients and mix till well combined.
- Pour the dressing over the mussels and serve.

Servings per Recipe: 6

Timing Information:

Preparation	30 m
Cooking	5 m
Total Time	35 m

Nutritional Information:

Calories	240 kcal
Fat	20.4 g
Carbohydrates	5.5g
Protein	9.1 g
Cholesterol	53 mg
Sodium	389 mg

* Percent Daily Values are based on a 2,000 calorie diet.

MUSSELS TRATTORIA STYLE

Ingredients

- 2 tbsp butter
- 4 cloves garlic, minced
- 1/2 tsp red pepper flakes, or to taste
- 1 lemon, zested
- 2 C. white wine
- freshly ground black pepper to taste

- 2 lb. mussels, cleaned and debearded
- 1 C. chopped fresh flat-leaf parsley
- 2 slices bread, grilled
- 2 lemon wedges for garnish

Directions

- In a large soup pan, melt the butter on medium heat and sauté for about 30 seconds.
- Stir in the lemon zest and red pepper flakes and sauté for about 45 seconds.
- Stir in the wine, salt and black pepper and bring to a boil.
- Stir in the mussels and cook, covered for about 1 minute.
- Uncover the pan and Stir the mussels and cook, covered for about 2 minutes.
- Stir in parsley and cook, covered for about 1-3 minutes.
- Serve with a topping of the lemon wedges alongside the grilled bread.

Servings per Recipe: 2

Timing Information:

Preparation	10 m
Cooking	10 m
Total Time	20 m

Nutritional Information:

Calories	553 kcal
Fat	14.8 g
Carbohydrates	40.5g
Protein	28.1 g
Cholesterol	91 mg
Sodium	620 mg

* Percent Daily Values are based on a 2,000 calorie diet.

SEAFOOD FETTUCCINI TOSCANO

Ingredients

- 1 (12 oz.) package fettuccini pasta
- 1 tbsp olive oil
- 1 onion, chopped
- 2 cloves garlic, minced
- 1 (16 oz.) can diced tomatoes
- 1 tsp tomato paste
- 5 fresh mushrooms, chopped
- 1 tsp dried basil
- 1/2 tsp dried oregano
- 1 tsp dried tarragon
- 36 raw green-lipped mussels
- 1/2 C. olives
- 2 fresh tomatoes, chopped

Directions

- In a large pan of boiling water, cook the pasta for about 8-10 minutes and drain well.
- Meanwhile in a large pan, heat the oil on medium heat and sauté the onion and garlic till tender.
- Stir in the remaining ingredients except the fresh tomatoes and olives.
- Simmer, covered for about 10 minutes.
- Stir in the fresh tomatoes and olives and simmer, covered for about 5 minutes.
- Pour mussels mixture over pasta and serve.

Servings per Recipe: 6

Timing Information:

Preparation	15 m
Cooking	20 m
Total Time	35 m

Nutritional Information:

Calories	310 kcal
Fat	5.5 g
Carbohydrates	50.3g
Protein	15.6 g
Cholesterol	16 mg
Sodium	325 mg

* Percent Daily Values are based on a 2,000 calorie diet.

CANADIAN MUSSELS COUNTRY STYLE

Ingredients

- 2 tbsp olive oil
- 1 onion, chopped
- 2 cloves garlic, minced
- 1 carrot, sliced
- 1 stalk celery, sliced
- 3 1/4 C. chicken broth
- 2 1/4 lb. mussels, cleaned and debearded
- 1 bunch fresh spinach, leaves torn in half

Directions

- In a large pan, heat the oil on medium heat and sauté the onion and garlic for about 5-7 minutes.
- Stir in the celery and carrot and cook for about 7-10 minutes.
- Add the broth and boil for about 5 minutes.
- Add the mussels and simmer, covered for about 5 minutes.
- Discard any unopened mussels.

Servings per Recipe: 4

Timing Information:

Preparation	20 m
Cooking	20 m
Total Time	40 m

Nutritional Information:

Calories	320 kcal
Fat	12.9 g
Carbohydrates	17.3g
Protein	33.4 g
Cholesterol	71 mg
Sodium	817 mg

* Percent Daily Values are based on a 2,000 calorie diet.

6-Ingredient Mussels Mediterranean

Ingredients

- 1 tbsp olive oil
- 4 shallots, thinly sliced
- 2 lb. mussels, cleaned and debearded
- 1/2 C. dry white wine
- 1 C. finely chopped Italian leaf parsley
- 1 C. Greek yogurt

Directions

- In a large pan, heat the oil on medium heat and sauté the shallots till tender.
- Increase the heat to high and add the mussels.
- Cook, covered for about 3-5 minutes.
- With a slotted spoon, transfer the mussels into serving plate.
- In the pan, add the parsley and wine and bring to a boil.
- Cook till the mixture reduces to the 1/3 of the total.
- Remove from the heat and stir in the yogurt.
- Place the yogurt sauce over mussels and serve.

Servings per Recipe: 4

Timing Information:

Preparation	5 m
Cooking	5 m
Total Time	20 m

Nutritional Information:

Calories	201 kcal
Fat	9.1 g
Carbohydrates	13.5g
Protein	11.5 g
Cholesterol	29 mg
Sodium	147 mg

* Percent Daily Values are based on a 2,000 calorie diet.

SANIBEL ISLAND STYLE MUSSELS

Ingredients

- 5 lb. mussels, cleaned and debearded
- 1 large onion, diced
- 1 (14.5 oz.) can diced tomatoes
- 5 large cloves garlic, chopped
- 1 (12 fluid oz.) can beer, or chicken broth
- 1/2 C. red wine
- 2 tbsp peppercorns in brine, crushed

Directions

- In a large pan of lightly salted water, soak the mussels for about 10 minutes and drain well.
- In another large pan, mix together the mussels and remaining ingredients and bring to a boil.
- Cook for about 10 minutes.
- Reduce the heat to low and simmer for about 5 minutes.
- Discard any unopened mussels.

Servings per Recipe: 4

Timing Information:

Preparation	15 m
Cooking	15 m
Total Time	40 m

Nutritional Information:

Calories	209 kcal
Fat	1.4 g
Carbohydrates	16.7g
Protein	19.1 g
Cholesterol	44 mg
Sodium	616 mg

* Percent Daily Values are based on a 2,000 calorie diet.

Oriental Steam Mussels

Ingredients

- 5 lb. fresh mussels, scrubbed and debearded
- 1/3 C. fresh lime juice
- 1 (13.5 oz.) can unsweetened coconut milk
- 1/3 C. dry white wine
- 1 1/2 tbsp Thai red curry paste
- 1 1/2 tbsp minced garlic
- 1 tbsp Asian fish sauce
- 1 tbsp white sugar
- 2 C. chopped fresh cilantro

Directions

- In a large pan, add all the ingredients except mussels and cilantro and stir till well combined.
- Bring to a boil on high heat and cook for about 2 minutes.
- Add mussels and cook, covered for about 5-8 minutes, stirring occasionally.
- Remove from the heat and discard any unopened mussels.
- Stir in the cilantro and serve.

Servings per Recipe: 6

Timing Information:

Preparation	20 m
Cooking	10 m
Total Time	30 m

Nutritional Information:

Calories	484 kcal
Fat	24.4 g
Carbohydrates	21.4g
Protein	48.3 g
Cholesterol	106 mg
Sodium	1353 mg

* Percent Daily Values are based on a 2,000 calorie diet.

How to Grill Mussels

Ingredients

- 3 tbsp butter, softened
- 2 cloves garlic, pressed
- 1 tsp curry powder
- 1/2 tsp ground cumin
- 1/8 tsp salt

- 2 lb. mussels, scrubbed and debearded
- 1 C. chopped red bell pepper
- 1/4 C. chopped fresh parsley
- 1 lime, thinly sliced
- 1 lime, cut into 4 wedges

Directions

- Set your grill to medium-high heat and grease the grill grate.
- In a bowl, mix together the butter, garlic, cumin, curry powder and salt.
- Place 4 large foil papers over a smooth surface.
- Place the mussels over foil papers evenly and place the butter mixture on top in the form of the dots.
- Top with the red bell pepper, parsley and lime slices.
- Tightly, wrap the foil around the mussels and cook over grill for about 5-10 minutes.
- Discard any unopened mussels.
- Serve the mussels with a garnishing of lime wedges.

Servings per Recipe: 4

Timing Information:

Preparation	20 m
Cooking	5 m
Total Time	25 m

Nutritional Information:

Calories	299 kcal
Fat	14.1 g
Carbohydrates	15.3g
Protein	28 g
Cholesterol	86 mg
Sodium	788 mg

* Percent Daily Values are based on a 2,000 calorie diet.

AMERICAN SEAFOOD BISQUE

Ingredients

- 2 lb. mussels, cleaned and debearded
- 1 1/4 C. white wine
- 1 1/2 C. water
- 3 tbsp butter
- 1 tbsp olive oil
- 1 onion, chopped
- 1 clove garlic, crushed
- 1 leek, bulb only, chopped
- 1/2 tsp fenugreek seeds, finely crushed
- 1 1/2 tbsp all-purpose flour
- 6 saffron threads
- 1 1/4 C. chicken broth
- 1 tbsp chopped fresh parsley
- salt and pepper to taste
- 2 tbsp whipping cream

Directions

- In a small bowl, mix together saffron threads and 1 tbsp of the boiling water.
- In a large pan, add the mussels, water and wine and cook, covered for about 6-7 minutes, shaking the pan occasionally.
- Remove from the heat and discard any unopened mussels.
- Through a fine sieve, strain the liquid and keep aside.
- In a pan, melt the butter and oil and sauté the onion, fenugreek, leek and garlic for about 5 minutes.
- Stir in the flour and cook for about 1 minute.

- Add about 2 1/2 C. of the strained liquid, broth and saffron mixture and bring to a boil.
- Simmer, covered for about 15 minutes.
- Meanwhile remove the mussels from the shells, keeping 8 still in the shells.
- Add all the mussels in the broth mixture with the remaining ingredients and cook for about 2-3 minutes.

Servings per Recipe: 6

Timing Information:

Preparation	35 m
Cooking	35 m
Total Time	1 h 10 m

Nutritional Information:

Calories	205 kcal
Fat	10.4 g
Carbohydrates	9g
Protein	9.7 g
Cholesterol	27 mg
Sodium	343 mg

* Percent Daily Values are based on a 2,000 calorie diet.

HEAVY CREAMED MUSSELS WITH CURRY

Ingredients

- 1/2 C. minced shallots
- 2 tbsp minced garlic
- 1 1/2 C. dry white wine
- 1 C. heavy cream
- 1 tsp curry powder

- 32 mussels - cleaned and debearded
- 1/4 C. butter
- 1/4 C. minced parsley
- 1/4 C. chopped green onions

Directions

- In a large pan, add the wine and bring to a gentle simmer.
- Add the garlic and shallots and sauté till tender.
- Stir in the curry powder and cream and add the mussels.
- Simmer, covered for a few minutes.
- With a slotted spoon, place the mussels in a bowl and discard any unopened mussels.
- Add the butter in the pan and stir to combine.
- Remove from the heat and immediately stir in the green onions and parsley.
- Pour sauce over mussels and serve.

Servings per Recipe: 4

Timing Information:

Preparation	40 m
Cooking	15 m
Total Time	55 m

Nutritional Information:

Calories	446 kcal
Fat	35.5 g
Carbohydrates	10.7g
Protein	6.4 g
Cholesterol	128 mg
Sodium	172 mg

* Percent Daily Values are based on a 2,000 calorie diet.

Maria's Seafood Marinara

Ingredients

- 1 tbsp olive oil
- 1 clove garlic, minced
- 1 (14.5 oz.) can crushed tomatoes
- 1/2 tsp dried oregano
- 1/2 tsp dried basil
- 1 pinch crushed red pepper flakes

- 1/4 C. white wine
- 1 lb. mussels, cleaned and debearded
- 8 oz. linguini pasta
- 1 lemon - cut into wedges, for garnish

Directions

- In a pan of lightly salted boiling water, cook the pasta for about 8-10 minutes and drain well.
- Meanwhile in a large pan, heat the oil on medium heat and sauté the garlic till tender. Stir in the tomatoes, herbs and red pepper flakes and reduce the heat to low. Simmer for about 5 minutes.
- Add the mussels and wine and increase the heat to high.
- Cook for about 3-5 minutes.
- Place the mussels mixture over pasta and drizzle with the lemon juice.
- Serve with a garnishing of the parsley and lemon wedges.

Servings per Recipe: 4

Timing Information:

Preparation	5 m
Cooking	15 m
Total Time	20 m

Nutritional Information:

Calories	304 kcal
Fat	5.4 g
Carbohydrates	52.8g
Protein	13 g
Cholesterol	9 mg
Sodium	188 mg

* Percent Daily Values are based on a 2,000 calorie diet.

San Francisco Mussels Soup

(Cioppino)

Ingredients

- 3/4 C. butter
- 2 onions, chopped
- 2 cloves garlic, minced
- 1 bunch fresh parsley, chopped
- 2 (14.5 oz.) cans stewed tomatoes
- 2 (14.5 oz.) cans chicken broth
- 2 bay leaves
- 1 tbsp dried basil
- 1/2 tsp dried thyme
- 1/2 tsp dried oregano
- 1 C. water
- 1 1/2 C. white wine
- 1 1/2 lb. large shrimp - peeled and deveined
- 1 1/2 lb. bay scallops
- 18 small clams
- 18 mussels, cleaned and debearded
- 1 1/2 C. crabmeat
- 1 1/2 lb. cod fillets, cubed

Directions

- In a large soup pan, melt the butter on medium-low heat and cook the onions, parsley and garlic till tender, stirring occasionally.
- Break the tomatoes in small pieces and add into pan with broth, wine, water, dried herbs and bay leaves.

- Simmer, covered for about 30 minutes.
- Stir in the seafood and bring to a boil.
- Reduce the heat and simmer for about 5-7 minutes.
- Serve hot alongside the warm crusty bread.

Servings per Recipe: 13

Timing Information:

Preparation	10 m
Cooking	45 m
Total Time	55 m

Nutritional Information:

Calories	318 kcal
Fat	12.9 g
Carbohydrates	9.3g
Protein	34.9 g
Cholesterol	164 mg
Sodium	755 mg

* Percent Daily Values are based on a 2,000 calorie diet.

Marseille Mussels Stew (Bouillabaisse)

Ingredients

- 3/4 C. olive oil
- 2 onions, thinly sliced
- 2 leeks, sliced
- 3 tomatoes - peeled, seeded and chopped
- 4 cloves garlic, minced
- 1 sprig fennel leaf
- 1 sprig fresh thyme
- 1 bay leaf
- 1 tsp orange zest
- 3/4 lb. mussels, cleaned and debearded
- 9 C. boiling water
- salt and pepper to taste
- 5 lb. sea bass
- 1 pinch saffron threads
- 3/4 lb. fresh shrimp, peeled and deveined

Directions

- In a large pan, heat the oil on low heat and sauté the leeks, onions, tomatoes and garlic till tender. Stir in the mussels, fennel, orange zest, thyme, bay leaf, salt, black pepper and boiling water and increase the heat to high.
- Boil for about 3 minutes. Stir in the fish and shrimp and reduce the heat to medium and simmer for about 12-15 minutes. Stir in the saffron and serve immediately.

Servings per Recipe: 12

Timing Information:

Preparation	15 m
Cooking	25 m
Total Time	40 m

Nutritional Information:

Calories	365 kcal
Fat	18 g
Carbohydrates	6g
Protein	42.9 g
Cholesterol	124 mg
Sodium	203 mg

* Percent Daily Values are based on a 2,000 calorie diet.

MUSSELS FRA DIAVOLO STEW

Ingredients

- 3 tbsp olive oil
- 2 lb. sea scallops
- 2 lb. large shrimp, peeled and deveined
- 1 lb. calamari rings
- 24 mussels, cleaned and debearded
- 24 littleneck clams, scrubbed and rinsed
- 3 (14.5 oz.) cans crushed tomatoes
- 1 C. water
- 2 (6.5 oz.) cans chopped clams
- 1/4 C. olive oil
- 1 small yellow onion, chopped
- 2 tbsp red pepper flakes
- 1 tbsp chopped garlic
- 1 tsp dried oregano
- 1 tsp dried parsley
- 1 tsp salt
- 2 (16 oz.) packages linguine pasta

Directions

- In a large skillet, heat 3 tbsp of the oil on medium heat and cook the shrimp, calamari rings and scallops for about 5 minutes.
- In another pan of boiling water, cook the littleneck clams and mussels and cook for about 3 minutes.
- Remove the mussels from the pan and rinse under hot water.

- Add the canned clams, crushed tomatoes, onion, garlic, herbs, salt, 1/4 C. of the oil and water and bring to a boil.
- Add the shrimp, calamari rings, scallops, littleneck clams and mussels and reduce the heat to low.
- Simmer for about 1 hour.
- During the last 10 minute cooking in a pan of lightly salted boiling water, cook the linguine for about 10 minutes.
- Drain well.
- Pour seafood mixture over sauce and serve.

Servings per Recipe: 10

Timing Information:

Preparation	30 m
Cooking	1 h 10 m
Total Time	1 h 40 m

Nutritional Information:

Calories	775 kcal
Fat	17.2 g
Carbohydrates	80.5g
Protein	72 g
Cholesterol	1329 mg
Sodium	1957 mg

* Percent Daily Values are based on a 2,000 calorie diet.

Parisian Restaurant Mussels

Ingredients

- 2 quarts mussels - cleaned and debearded
- 2 tbsp butter
- 2 large onion, peeled and sliced into rings
- 3 stalks celery, cut into 1/2 inch pieces
- 1 1/2 C. dry white wine
- 2 sprigs fresh thyme
- 2 bay leaves
- salt and pepper to taste
- 1/2 C. creme fraiche
- 1/4 C. chopped fresh parsley

Directions

- In a large pan, melt the butter till it just become brown.
- Stir in the celery and onion and cook till tender.
- Stir in the mussels and cook for a few minutes.
- Stir in the wine, bay leaves, thyme sprigs, salt and black pepper and cook for about 10 minutes.
- Stir in the 2 large spoons of the crème fraiche.
- Serve with a topping of the parsley and dollop of crème fraiche.

Servings per Recipe: 4

Timing Information:

Preparation	30 m
Cooking	20 m
Total Time	50 m

Nutritional Information:

Calories	316 kcal
Fat	17.8 g
Carbohydrates	13g
Protein	11.3 g
Cholesterol	79 mg
Sodium	504 mg

* Percent Daily Values are based on a 2,000 calorie diet.

CHICAGO TOWN BRAISED MUSSELS

Ingredients

- 1 tbsp olive oil
- 2 shallots, finely chopped
- 4 cloves garlic, finely chopped
- 1 bulb fennel - trimmed, cored and thinly sliced
- 1 large tomato, cubed
- 1/2 C. white wine
- 1/4 C. ouzo (Greek liquor) or chicken broth
- 1/2 C. heavy cream
- 4 lb. mussels, cleaned and debearded
- 1/3 C. fresh basil leaves, torn
- salt to taste

Directions

- In a large pan, heat the oil on medium heat and sauté the shallots and garlic till tender.
- Stir in the tomato and fennel and cook for about 5 minutes.
- Stir in the heavy cream, ouzo and white wine and bring to a boil.
- Add the mussels, half of the basil and salt and cook, covered for about 5 minutes.
- Serve with a garnishing of the remaining basil.

Servings per Recipe: 4

Timing Information:

Preparation	15 m
Cooking	5 m
Total Time	30 m

Nutritional Information:

Calories	286 kcal
Fat	15.7 g
Carbohydrates	15.7g
Protein	16.3 g
Cholesterol	76 mg
Sodium	245 mg

* Percent Daily Values are based on a 2,000 calorie diet.

Maria's Paella
(One Pan Dinner)

Ingredients

- 2 1/2 C. uncooked white rice, rinsed and drained
- 6 C. chicken stock, divided
- 3 cloves garlic
- 1 tsp chopped fresh parsley
- 1/2 tsp curry powder
- 5 saffron threads
- salt and ground black pepper to taste
- 1/4 C. olive oil
- 1 onion, diced
- 1 (3 lb.) whole chicken, cut into small pieces
- 2 C. peeled and deveined small shrimp, diced
- 6 small lobster tails
- 1/2 lb. clams in shell, scrubbed
- 1 (8 oz.) jar mushrooms, drained
- 1 C. green peas
- 1 (2 oz.) can mussels

Directions

- In a pan, add the broth and bring to a boil on medium-high heat.
- Reduce the heat to low and keep the pan covered on heat.
- With a mortar and pestle, puree a smooth liquid with 1/2 C. of the broth, parsley, garlic, saffron threads, curry powder, salt and black pepper.

- In a paella pan, heat the oil on medium-high heat and sauté the onion till browned.
- Stir in the lobster, clams, shrimp and chicken and cook for about 10 minutes.
- Stir in the smooth broth mixture, rice and the remaining broth and simmer for about 15 minutes.
- Stir in the mussels, peas and shrimp and simmer for about 10 minutes.
- Remove from the heat and keep aside, covered for about 7 minutes.

Servings per Recipe: 8

Timing Information:

Preparation	50 m
Cooking	45 m
Total Time	1 h 45 m

Nutritional Information:

Calories	591 kcal
Fat	21.8 g
Carbohydrates	54g
Protein	42 g
Cholesterol	153 mg
Sodium	1032 mg

* Percent Daily Values are based on a 2,000 calorie diet.

OREGON POTATO HOT POT

Ingredients

- 2 lb. Yukon Gold potatoes, peeled and cubed
- 1/2 lb. broccoli rabe, thick stems peeled
- 1/2 C. olive oil
- 4 anchovy filets, rinsed and chopped
- 4 cloves garlic, minced
- 2 1/2 lb. mussels, cleaned and debearded
- 2 tbsp chopped fresh parsley
- 1/2 C. water
- salt to taste

Directions

- In a large pan of water cook the potatoes with the salt for about 15 minutes, then drain well.
- In a pan of salted boiling water, cook the broccoli rabe till just tender.
- Drain well and chop into 2-inch pieces in lengthwise.
- In a large deep skillet, add the oil, garlic and anchovies on high heat.
- Cook for about 1 minute, mashing the anchovies with the back of the spoon.
- Arrange the mussels in the skillet and place the potatoes, broccoli and parsley on top.
- Add the water and salt and cook, covered till mussels have opened.

Servings per Recipe: 10

Timing Information:

Preparation	30 m
Cooking	45 m
Total Time	1 h 15 m

Nutritional Information:

Calories	199 kcal
Fat	11.3 g
Carbohydrates	18.5g
Protein	6.6 g
Cholesterol	10 mg
Sodium	121 mg

* Percent Daily Values are based on a 2,000 calorie diet.

ROASTED MUSSELS AND CLAMS

Ingredients

- 8 medium red potatoes, scrubbed
- 1 lb. clams in shell, scrubbed
- 1 lb. mussels, cleaned and debearded
- 1/2 lb. unpeeled large shrimp
- 1 (48 fluid oz.) can chicken broth
- 1/4 C. dry vermouth
- 1 1/2 C. butter, divided
- 1 loaf French bread

Directions

- In the bottom of a large pan, arrange the layers of the potatoes, clams, mussels and shrimp.
- Add the vermouth and enough broth that fills the pan halfway.
- Chop the half the butter over the seafood.
- With a lid, cover the pan and then tightly, seal with a foil paper.
- Bring to a boil and reduce the heat to medium-low.
- Simmer for about 45 minutes.
- Remove from the heat and transfer the seafood mixture into serving dishes.
- Serve with a topping of the remaining softened bread alongside the bred.

Servings per Recipe: 4

Timing Information:

Preparation	20 m
Cooking	45 m
Total Time	1 h 5 m

Nutritional Information:

Calories	1383 kcal
Fat	74.1 g
Carbohydrates	1137.4g
Protein	41.6 g
Cholesterol	294 mg
Sodium	3133 mg

* Percent Daily Values are based on a 2,000 calorie diet.

MUSSELS MILANESE

Ingredients

- 1 1/4 lbs mussels, cleaned and debearded
- 2 tbsp butter
- 1 1/2 tbsp onions, minced
- 1 garlic clove, minced
- 1 small tomatoes, chopped
- 1/4 tsp oregano
- salt & freshly ground black pepper (to taste)
- 1/4 C. dry white wine

Directions

- In a large bowl of salted water, soak the mussels with flour for about 30 minutes. With a brush, clean the mussels and place in another bowl of clean water. With a paper towel, pat dry the mussels.
- In a large pan, melt the butter and sauté the onion till tender.
- Stir in the garlic and sauté for about 1 minute.
- Stir in the tomato, salt, black pepper and oregano and cook till the tomatoes become tender. Stir in the wine and bring to a boil.
- Add the mussels and simmer, covered for about 4 minutes.
- Uncover and stir the mussels and simmer, covered for about 2-4 minutes.
- Discard any unopened mussels.
- Serve immediately.

Servings per Recipe: 2

Timing Information:

Preparation	45 mins
Total Time	1 hr

Nutritional Information:

Calories	383.8
Fat	17.9g
Cholesterol	110.1mg
Sodium	918.5mg
Carbohydrates	14.2g
Protein	34.5g

* Percent Daily Values are based on a 2,000 calorie diet.

CURRY CAMBODIAN MUSSELS

Ingredients

- 1/4 C. butter
- 5 plum tomatoes, seeded and chopped
- 2 tbsp minced garlic
- 1 tbsp peeled fresh ginger, minced
- 2 (14 oz.) cans unsweetened coconut milk
- 1 tbsp Thai red curry paste (more if you like)
- 7 tbsp chopped fresh cilantro, divided
- 1 tsp salt
- 3 lbs mussels, scrubbed and debearded

Directions

- In a large pan, melt the butter on medium heat and sauté the tomatoes, ginger and garlic for about 2 minutes.
- Stir in the coconut milk, 4 tbsp of the cilantro, curry paste and salt and simmer for about 4 minutes.
- Add the mussels and simmer, covered for about 5 minutes.
- Discard any unopened mussels.
- Serve with a garnishing of the remaining cilantro.

Servings per Recipe: 4

Timing Information:

Preparation	40 mins
Total Time	51 mins

Nutritional Information:

Calories	807.7
Fat	61.6g
Cholesterol	126.0mg
Sodium	1689.4mg
Carbohydrates	22.9g
Protein	45.7g

* Percent Daily Values are based on a 2,000 calorie diet.

MUSSELS FLORENTINE

Ingredients

- 12 garlic cloves, minced
- 1 1/2 tsp hot red pepper flakes
- 1/2 C. olive oil
- 1 (28 oz.) cans whole tomatoes
- 2 tbsp tomato paste
- 2 tsp dried oregano
- 1 tsp dried basil
- 1/4 C. capers, drained
- 1/2 C. kalamata olive, pitted and chopped
- 1/3 C. red wine
- 3 lbs mussels, cleaned and debearded
- 1 lb linguine, cooked

Directions

- In a large skillet, heat the oil and stir in the red pepper flakes and garlic.
- Stir in the remaining ingredients except the mussels and linguine and simmer for about 15 minutes.
- Meanwhile prepare the linguine according to package's directions, then drain well.
- Increase the heat to medium.
- Add the mussels and simmer, covered for about 3-6 minutes.
- Discard any unopened mussels.
- Pour the mussels mixture over linguine and serve.

Servings per Recipe: 6

Timing Information:

Preparation	10 mins
Total Time	35 mins

Nutritional Information:

Calories	702.7
Fat	25.8g
Cholesterol	63.6mg
Sodium	958.7mg
Carbohydrates	75.4g
Protein	39.1g

* Percent Daily Values are based on a 2,000 calorie diet.

FRIED MUSSELS

Ingredients

- 14 mussels
- 2 eggs
- 2 tbsp flour
- 1 tsp baking powder
- 2 tbsp parsley, chopped

- 2 tbsp basil, fresh, chopped
- 1/2 tsp salt
- black pepper, freshly ground
- butter, for frying

Directions

- Steam the mussels till they just begin to pen.
- Remove the mussels from the shells and chop them roughly.
- In a bowl, crack the eggs and beat well.
- Sift together the flour and baking powder in the bowl of eggs and beat till well combined.
- Add the mussels, herbs, salt and black pepper and stir to combine.
- In a skillet, melt the butter and add the desired amount of the mixture.
- Cook from both sides till golden brown.

Servings per Recipe: 6

Timing Information:

| Preparation | 10 mins |
| Total Time | 15 mins |

Nutritional Information:

Calories	67.1
Fat	2.5g
Cholesterol	80.9mg
Sodium	385.2mg
Carbohydrates	3.8g
Protein	6.8g

* Percent Daily Values are based on a 2,000 calorie diet.

How to Make Mussel Vinaigrette

Ingredients

- 24 medium mussels, cleaned and debearded
- 1/2 C. olive oil
- 3 tbsp red wine vinegar
- 1 tsp capers, chopped if large
- 1 tbsp minced onion
- 1 tbsp minced pimiento
- 1 tbsp minced parsley
- salt
- fresh ground pepper
- 1 slice lemon

Directions

- Discard the mussels that do not close tightly.
- In a bowl, add the vinegar and oil and beat well.
- Add the remaining ingredients except the lemon slice and neat till well combined.
- In a pan, add the mussels, 1 C. of the water and lemon slice and bring to a boil.
- Cook till the mussels are opened.
- Remove from the heat and let them cool.
- Remove the half of mussels from the shells and mix in the vinaigrette.
- Pour the vinaigrette over the mussels in the shells and serve.

Servings per Recipe: 24

Timing Information:

Preparation	20 mins
Total Time	40 mins

Nutritional Information:

Calories	54.3
Fat	4.8g
Cholesterol	4.4mg
Sodium	50.8mg
Carbohydrates	0.7g
Protein	1.9g

* Percent Daily Values are based on a 2,000 calorie diet.

GINGER BASIL MUSSELS

Ingredients

- 1/2 can coconut milk
- 1/4 C. peeled sliced ginger
- 1 tbsp sugar
- 2 tbsp lemon juice
- 2 tsp curry powder
- 1 can chicken broth
- 2 lbs mussels
- 1/4 C. fresh basil, chiffonaded

Directions

- In a large pan mix together all the ingredients except the mussels and basil, then bring to a boil.
- Add the mussels and simmer, covered for about 5 minutes.
- Discard any unopened mussels.
- Serve with a garnishing of the basil.

Servings per Recipe: 2

Timing Information:

| Preparation | 10 mins |
| Total Time | 20 mins |

Nutritional Information:

Calories	508.8
Fat	12.6g
Cholesterol	127.3mg
Sodium	2212.1mg
Carbohydrates	34.0g
Protein	61.5g

* Percent Daily Values are based on a 2,000 calorie diet.

Saucy Spanish Mussels

Ingredients

- 1 tbsp olive oil
- 1 large onion, chopped
- 1 tbsp minced garlic
- 1 (16 oz.) cans diced tomatoes
- 1/2 C. minced parsley
- pepper
- 1 C. dry white wine
- 4 lbs cleaned mussels

Directions

- In a large pan, heat the oil and sauté the onion and garlic for about 5 minutes.
- Stir in the parsley, tomatoes and black pepper and cook for about 2 minutes.
- Stir in the wine and cook for about 2 minutes.
- Add the mussels and simmer, covered for about 3-4 minutes, stirring occasionally.
- Discard any unopened mussels.
- Serve with a topping of the French crusty bread.

Servings per Recipe: 4

Timing Information:

Preparation	15 mins
Total Time	27 mins

Nutritional Information:

Calories	510.3
Fat	13.9g
Cholesterol	127.3mg
Sodium	1315.3mg
Carbohydrates	27.3g
Protein	55.9g

* Percent Daily Values are based on a 2,000 calorie diet.

Mussels Martinique

Ingredients

- 4 C. mussels
- 2 tbsp extra virgin olive oil
- 2 tbsp yellow onions, chopped
- 2 tbsp garlic, chopped
- 2 tbsp Pernod
- 1 tbsp fresh basil, chopped
- 1/2 lemon, juice and pulp of

Lemon Butter Sauce (use 3/4 C.)

- 1/4 C. real butter
- 2 tbsp yellow onions, minced
- 2 tbsp garlic, minced
- 1/3 C. fresh lemon juice
- 2 tbsp dry white wine
- kosher salt
- white pepper, to taste
- 2 tbsp cold butter

Directions

- For lemon butter sauce in a frying pan, melt the butter on low heat.
- Remove from the heat and keep aside till the milk solids settle to the bottom.
- Discard the milk solids. In a skillet, heat the 2 tbsp of the clarified butter and sauté the onion and garlic till tender.
- Stir in the salt, black pepper, wine and lemon juice and simmer for about 2-3 minutes.
- Remove from the heat and stir in the cold butter.
- Meanwhile in a bowl of cold water, soak the mussels for about 8 minutes.
- With a sharp knife, remove the beards and rinse under cold water.

- In a skillet, heat the oil and cook the mussels, covered for about 2-6 minutes.
- Stir in the onion and garlic and cook, covered for about 1 minute.
- Stir in the lemon butter, Pernod, basil and lemon juice and cook for about 45 seconds.
- Discard any unopened mussels.
- Serve immediately.

Servings per Recipe: 2

Timing Information:

Preparation	15 mins
Total Time	30 mins

Nutritional Information:

Calories	740.7
Fat	55.0g
Cholesterol	175.5mg
Sodium	1167.3mg
Carbohydrates	23.0g
Protein	37.7g

* Percent Daily Values are based on a 2,000 calorie diet.

Mussels Toscano

Ingredients

- 2 1/4 lbs mussels, cleaned
- 1/2 C. dry white wine
- 2 green onions, chopped
- 2 -3 garlic cloves, minced
- 1/4 C. fresh dill, chopped plus extra to garnish
- 1/4 C. fresh parsley
- 1/4 tsp dried red chili pepper
- 2 ripe plum tomatoes, chopped
- 2 tbsp butter

Directions

- In a large pan, add the mussels and wine on high heat and bring to a boil.
- Cook, covered for a few minutes, stirring continuously.
- Stir in the remaining ingredients except the butter and cook, covered for about 3-4 minutes on medium-high heat.
- Stir in the butter and remove from the heat.
- Serve with a garnishing of the dill.

Servings per Recipe: 2

Timing Information:

Preparation	15 mins
Total Time	15 mins

Nutritional Information:

Calories	614.5
Fat	23.2g
Cholesterol	173.7mg
Sodium	1558.8mg
Carbohydrates	25.5g
Protein	62.3g

* Percent Daily Values are based on a 2,000 calorie diet.

CREAMY DIJON MUSSELS

Ingredients

- 2 -3 tbsp butter
- 1/4 C. finely chopped onion
- 2 tbsp finely chopped shallots
- 1 tsp finely chopped garlic
- 3 lbs mussels, beards removed, cleaned and scrubbed
- sea salt
- fresh ground pepper
- 1 bay leaf
- 2 sprigs fresh thyme
- 1/4 C. dry white wine
- 1/2 C. heavy cream
- 2 tbsp Dijon mustard
- 2 tbsp finely chopped flat leaf parsley

Directions

- In a large pan, melt the butter and sauté the shallots onions and garlic till soft.
- Stir in the remaining ingredients except the mustard and thyme and bring to a boil. Reduce the heat to medium and simmer, covered for about 5 minutes, shaking the pan occasionally. With a slotted spoon, transfer the mussels into a bowl and discard any unopened mussels. Cover with a foil paper to keep them warm. Cook the sauce for about 1 minute and discard the thyme and bay leaf.
- Add the mustard, beating continuously till heated completely.
- Pour the sauce over the mussels and serve with a garnishing of the parsley alongside the crusty bread.

Servings per Recipe: 4

Timing Information:

Preparation	10 mins
Total Time	25 mins

Nutritional Information:

Calories	473.5
Fat	24.6g
Cholesterol	151.5mg
Sodium	1114.4mg
Carbohydrates	16.6g
Protein	41.8g

* Percent Daily Values are based on a 2,000 calorie diet.

Topped Mussel Platter

Ingredients

- 1 C. onion (diced)
- 2 tbsp extra virgin olive oil
- 4 tbsp garlic (minced)
- 1/2 tsp red pepper flakes
- 1 bay leaf
- 1 tsp salt
- 1 tsp black pepper
- 4 oz. tomatoes (diced)
- 1 tsp basil
- 1 1/2 C. wine
- 2 lbs mussels

Directions

- In a large bowl of cold water, add the mussels and 2 tbsp of the flour.
- Keep aside for about 10-15 minutes, then rinse under the cold water.
- In a large skillet, heat the oil and sauté the onion, , garlic, bay leaf and red pepper flakes for about 6-10 minutes.
- Stir in the tomatoes, basil, salt and black pepper and cook for about 3 minutes.
- Add mussels and wine cook till all the mussels have opened.
- Serve alongside the crusty bread.

Servings per Recipe: 2

Timing Information:

Preparation	15 mins
Total Time	45 mins

Nutritional Information:

Calories	732.2
Fat	24.0g
Cholesterol	127.3mg
Sodium	2481.1mg
Carbohydrates	38.4g
Protein	56.7g

* Percent Daily Values are based on a 2,000 calorie diet.

COUNTRY STYLE MUSSELS WITH LEEKS

Ingredients

- 3 medium leeks, cleaned and roughly chopped
- 3 garlic cloves, finely diced
- 2 tbsp olive oil
- 2 tbsp butter
- 3 oz. white wine
- 1/4 pint heavy cream
- 2 1/2 lbs mussels, cleaned
- 1/4 C. parsley, roughly chopped

Directions

- In a large pan, heat the oil and butter and sauté the garlic and leeks for about 5 minutes.
- Stir in the wine and increase the heat and cook for about 1 minute.
- Stir in the cream and bring to a boil.
- Add the mussels and cook, covered till all the mussels have opened.
- Discard any unopened mussels.
- Serve alongside crusty bread.

Servings per Recipe: 4

Timing Information:

Preparation	25 mins
Total Time	40 mins

Nutritional Information:

Calories	528.1
Fat	30.1g
Cholesterol	135.6mg
Sodium	892.3mg
Carbohydrates	22.5g
Protein	35.7g

* Percent Daily Values are based on a 2,000 calorie diet.

Mussels Marrakesh

Ingredients

- 1 medium onion, coarsely chopped
- 2 garlic cloves, thinly sliced
- 1 1/4 tsp ground cumin
- 1 tsp paprika
- 1 tsp ground ginger
- 3/8 tsp ground cinnamon
- 1/8 tsp cayenne
- 3 tbsp olive oil
- 1 tbsp cider vinegar
- 1 (15 oz.) cans chickpeas, drained and rinsed
- 2 tsp sugar
- 1 (28 oz.) cans whole tomatoes with juice, juice reserved and tomatoes coarsely chopped
- 3 lbs mussels, scrubbed and beards removed
- 2 tbsp fresh flat-leaf parsley, chopped

Directions

- In a large heavy pan, heat the oil on medium-low heat and sauté the onion and garlic for about 6 minutes. Add the vinegar and simmer for about 1 minute. Stir in the sugar, chickpeas, tomatoes and reserved juice and increase the heat to medium. Simmer, stirring occasionally for about 15 minutes.
- Add the mussels and simmer, covered for about 3-6 minutes.
- Discard any unopened mussels. Stir in the parsley and serve.

Servings per Recipe: 4

Timing Information:

Preparation	15 mins
Total Time	45 mins

Nutritional Information:

Calories	590.5
Fat	19.6g
Cholesterol	95.5mg
Sodium	1728.0mg
Carbohydrates	55.7g
Protein	48.0g

* Percent Daily Values are based on a 2,000 calorie diet.

FLORIDA MUSSEL SOUP

Ingredients

- 30 fresh mussels (scrub and debeard)
- 2 garlic cloves, crushed
- 1 onion, peeled and chopped
- 2 tbsp olive oil
- 2 tbsp parsley, chopped
- 1 tsp chopped fresh chili pepper
- 2 tbsp lemon juice
- 3/4 C. dry white wine
- 1 1/2 C. water
- 400 g crushed tomatoes with juice
- salt and black pepper

Directions

- In a large pan, heat the oil and sauté the onion and garlic till tender.
- Stir in the chili pepper and parsley and sauté for about 1-2 minutes.
- Add the water, wine and lemon juice and increase the heat.
- Bring to a boil and reduce the heat to medium.
- Simmer, covered for about 5 minutes.
- Discard any unopened mussels.
- Discard the top shell from each mussel.
- Season with the salt and black pepper and remove from the heat.

Servings per Recipe: 4

Timing Information:

Preparation	15 mins
Total Time	35 mins

Nutritional Information:

Calories	241.9
Fat	9.6g
Cholesterol	33.6mg
Sodium	566.5mg
Carbohydrates	15.9g
Protein	15.5g

* Percent Daily Values are based on a 2,000 calorie diet.

CREAMY CITY MUSSELS

Ingredients

- 6 tbsp butter
- 4 garlic cloves, minced
- 4 shallots, minced
- 1/4 C. parsley, chopped
- 6 tbsp lemon juice
- 3 tomatoes, seeded and diced small
- 4 lbs mussels
- 3/4 C. dry white wine
- 1 C. heavy whipping cream
- 1 lemon, zested and cut into slices
- Garnish
- chopped parsley

Directions

- In a bowl, mix together the shallot, garlic, 1 tbsp of the parsley, 1/4 C. of the lemon juice, butter, salt and black pepper.
- In a Dutch oven, melt the butter on medium heat and sauté till shallots become tender. Add the mussels and stir for about 1 minute.
- Stir in the 3/4 C. of the cream, wine, lemon peel, salt and black pepper.
- Place the tomato and lemon slices on top and simmer, covered for about 8-10 minutes. With a slotted spoon, transfer the mussels into a bowl and discard any unopened mussels. Cook the sauce for about 5 minutes.
- Add the parsley and remaining lemon juice and cream.
- Boil for about 1 minute and pour over the mussels. Serve immediately.

Servings per Recipe: 2

Timing Information:

| Preparation | 15 mins |
| Total Time | 35 mins |

Nutritional Information:

Calories	1667.2
Fat	99.6g1
Cholesterol	509.2mg
Sodium	2917.5mg
Carbohydrates	65.3g
Protein	115.1g

* Percent Daily Values are based on a 2,000 calorie diet.

BARCELONA BROWN RICE PAELLA

Ingredients

- 1 lb extra-large shrimp, peeled and deveined
- salt & freshly ground black pepper
- olive oil
- 8 -9 medium garlic cloves
- 1 lb chicken thigh
- 1 red bell pepper, seeded and cut pole to pole into 1/2-inch-wide strips
- 8 oz. spanish chorizo, sliced 1/2 inch thick on the bias
- 1 medium onion, chopped fine
- 1 (14 1/2 oz.) cans diced tomatoes, drained, minced, and drained again
- 2 C. long grain brown rice
- 3 C. low chicken broth
- 1/3 C. dry white wine
- 1/2 tsp saffron thread, crumbled
- 1 bay leaf
- 1 dozen mussels, scrubbed and debearded
- 1/2 C. frozen green pea, thawed
- 2 tsp fresh parsley leaves
- 1 lemon, cut into wedges, for serving

Directions

- Set your oven to 350 degrees F before doing anything else and arrange the oven rack to lower-middle position.

- In s bowl, add the shrimp, 1 tsp of the garlic, 1 tbsp of the oil, salt and black pepper and toss to coat well.
- Refrigerate, covered till serving.
- In another bowl, add the chicken and season with the salt and black pepper.
- In a large Dutch oven, heat 2 tsp of the oil on medium-high heat and sauté the peppers for about 3-4 minutes.
- Transfer the peppers into a plate.
- In the same pan, heat 1 tsp of the oil and cook the chicken for about 3 minutes. Transfer the chicken into another plate.
- Reduce the heat to medium and cook the chorizo for about 4-5 minutes.
- Transfer the chorizo in the plate with the chicken.
- In the same Dutch oven, heat 2 tbsp of the oil on medium heat and sauté the onion for about 3 minutes.
- Add the remaining garlic and sauté for about 1 minute.
- Add the tomatoes and cook for about 3 minutes.
- Add the rice and stir fry for about 1-2 minutes.
- Add the wine, broth, saffron, bay leaf and salt and bring to a boil on medium-high heat. Cover and cook in the oven for about 30 minutes.
- Stir in the chicken and chorizo, cover and cook in the oven for about 15 minutes. Insert the mussels in rice mixture, hinged side down and place the shrimp over rice.
- Top with the peppers, cover and cook in the oven for about 12 minutes.
- Remove from the oven and keep aside, covered for about 5 minutes before serving.
- Serve hot with a garnishing of parsley and lemon wedges.

Servings per Recipe: 6

Timing Information:

Preparation	20 mins
Total Time	1 hr 8 mins

Nutritional Information:

Calories	747.5
Cholesterol	220.7mg
Sodium	933.3mg
Carbohydrates	64.3g
Protein	50.6g

* Percent Daily Values are based on a 2,000 calorie diet.

Seafood Au Gratin

Ingredients

- 1 lb fresh mussels, cleaned and debearded
- 1 tbsp butter
- 1 tbsp olive oil
- 3 tbsp parmesan cheese
- 2 tbsp chopped parsley
- 2 cloves garlic
- salt & freshly ground black pepper

Directions

- Set the broiler of your oven to 500 degrees F.
- In a large pan of water, add the mussels and simmer, covered for about 5 minutes.
- Drain well and discard any unopened mussels.
- Discard the top half shell from each mussel.
- In a bowl, mix togerher the remaining ingredients.
- In an oven proof dish, arranger the mussels in a single layer.
- Divide the cheese mixture over the mussels and cook under the broiler for about 2-3 minutes.
- Serve with the crusty bread.

Servings per Recipe: 4

Timing Information:

Preparation	15 mins
Total Time	22 mins

Nutritional Information:

Calories	172.0
Fat	9.8g
Cholesterol	42.7mg
Sodium	408.9mg
Carbohydrates	4.9g
Protein	15.1g

* Percent Daily Values are based on a 2,000 calorie diet.

Greek Fried Cheese Pan (Seafood Saganaki)

Ingredients

- 1 1/2 lbs black mussels, cleaned and debearded
- 1/2 C. dry white wine
- 3 sprigs fresh thyme
- 1 bay leaf
- 1 tbsp olive oil
- 1 large onion, finely chopped
- 1 garlic clove, finely chopped
- 14 oz. ripe tomatoes, peeled and very finely chopped
- 2 tbsp tomato paste
- 1/2 tsp sugar
- 1 tbsp red wine vinegar
- 2 1/4 oz. feta cheese, crumbled
- 1 tsp fresh thyme leave

Directions

- In a large pan, add the wine, bay leaf and thyme and bring to a boil.
- Add the mussels and simmer, covered for about 4-5 minutes.
- With a slotted spoon, transfer the mussels in a bowl and discard any unopened mussels.
- Discard the top half shell from each mussel.
- Strain the cooking liquid in a bowl.

- In a pan, heat the oil on medium heat and sauté the onion and garlic for about 3 minutes.
- Stir in the garlic and sauté for about 1 minute.
- Stir in the reserved cooking liquid and increase the heat, then bring to a boil.
- Boil for about 2 minutes and stir in the sugar, tomatoes and tomato paste.
- Simmer for about 5 minutes and add the mussels on medium heat.
- Cook for about 1 minute.
- Serve with a topping of the feta and thyme.

Servings per Recipe: 6

Timing Information:

Preparation	35 mins
Total Time	1 hr

Nutritional Information:

Calories	192.6
Fat	7.3g
Cholesterol	41.8mg
Sodium	499.0mg
Carbohydrates	11.6g
Protein	16.2g

* Percent Daily Values are based on a 2,000 calorie diet.

Mussels Neapolitan

Ingredients

- 2 lbs mussels, cleaned and debearded
- 1 C. white wine
- 1/2 C. salted butter
- 5 garlic cloves, coarsely chopped
- 2 tbsp olive oil
- 1 tbsp parsley paste
- 1 tbsp italian seasoning
- 1/8 tsp crushed red pepper flakes
- 1/4 tsp salt
- 1/4 tsp black pepper

Directions

- In a nonstick pan, heat the oil and sauté the garlic till tender.
- Meanwhile in a large pan, add the mussels, butter, wine and cooked garlic and simmer, covered on medium heat.
- Discard any unopened mussels.
- Stir in the remaining ingredients and simmer for about 2 minutes.
- Serve with the bread.

Servings per Recipe: 4

Timing Information:

Preparation	10 mins
Total Time	20 mins

Nutritional Information:

Calories	512.9
Fat	34.8g
Cholesterol	124.6mg
Sodium	1002.0mg
Carbohydrates	11.2g
Protein	27.6g

* Percent Daily Values are based on a 2,000 calorie diet.

Latin Chorizo Mussel Spaghetti

Ingredients

- coarse salt
- 1 lb spaghetti
- 2 tbsp extra virgin olive oil
- 1/2 lb chorizo sausage, cut in half lengthwise, then sliced into half-moons
- 1 small red onion, chopped
- 3 garlic cloves, chopped
- 1 celery rib, finely chopped
- 1 small carrot, peeled and finely chopped
- 1 tbsp fresh thyme leave, chopped
- coarse black pepper
- 1 C. dry white wine
- 1 (15 oz.) cans diced fire-roasted tomatoes (Muir Glen brand)
- 1 lb mussels, scrubbed
- 1/2 C. fresh flat leaf parsley, coarsely chopped
- crusty bread

Directions

- In a large pan of lightly salted boiling water, cook the pasta according to package's directions.
- Drain well.
- Meanwhile, in a large skillet, heat oil on medium heat.
- Add chorizo and cook for about 2 minutes.
- Stir in the carrots, onion, celery, garlic, thyme, salt and black pepper and cook for about 5 minutes.

- Stir in the tomatoes and wine and bring to a gentle simmer.
- Add in the mussels and cook, tightly covered for about 4-6 minutes.
- With a slotted spoon, place the mussels in a bowl and cover with foil paper to keep them warm.
- In the skillet, add the pasta and parsley and toss to coat well.
- Cook for about 1 minute.
- Place the pasta mixture in serving plates and top with the mussels.
- Serve alongside crusty bread.

Servings per Recipe: 4

Timing Information:

Preparation	30 mins
Total Time	44 mins

Nutritional Information:

Calories	907.7
Fat	32.8g
Cholesterol	81.7mg
Sodium	1055.9mg
Carbohydrates	96.5g
Protein	42.8g

* Percent Daily Values are based on a 2,000 calorie diet.

Pacific Northwest Creamy Mussel Soup

Ingredients

- 5 lbs mussels, in shells, cleaned and debearded
- 1 C. dry white wine or 1 C. water
- 1 lb thin-skinned potato
- 1 onion (1/2 lb.)
- 1 stalk celery (3 oz.)
- 2 tbsp butter or 2 tbsp margarine
- 2 tsp curry powder
- 1 1/2 tsp dried basil
- 1 (28 oz.) cans tomato sauce
- 2 C. whipping cream
- salt and pepper

Directions

- Discard the mussels that will not close after a light tap
- In a large pan, add the mussels and wine on high heat and bring to a boil.
- Reduce the heat to medium and simmer, covered for about 5-8 minutes.
- Arrange a strainer over a large bowl and drain the mussels, reserving the liquid in the bowl. In the same pan, melt the butter on medium heat and cook the celery and onion for about 6-8 minutes, stirring occasionally.
- Stir in the basil and curry powder and cook for about 30 seconds.
- Stir in the reserved cooking liquid, potatoes, cream and tomato sauce and increase the heat to high. Bring to a boil and then reduce the heat to low.
- Simmer, covered for about 30 minutes, stirring occasionally.

- Remove the mussels from the shells and add in the soup.
- Simmer for about 3-5 minutes.
- Season with the salt and black pepper and serve.

Servings per Recipe: 8

Timing Information:

Preparation	30 mins
Total Time	1 hr 10 mins

Nutritional Information:

Calories	575.1
Fat	31.5g
Cholesterol	168.7mg
Sodium	1394.6mg
Carbohydrates	29.9g
Protein	37.8g

* Percent Daily Values are based on a 2,000 calorie diet.

European Mussels Chowder

Ingredients

- 1 kg mussels, in shells
- 2 onions, medium (cubed)
- 1 tbsp canola oil
- 1 carrot, large (cubed)
- 2 celery ribs, large (cubed)
- 2 potatoes, medium size (cubed)
- 50 g butter
- ½ C. flour, standard (plain)
- 2 C. milk
- 2 C. fish stock
- salt and pepper
- parsley, chopped

Directions

- In a large pan, add 2 C. of the water and bring to a boil.
- Add the mussels and cook till all the mussels have opened.
- With a slotted spoon, transfer the mussels into a bowl.
- Remove the mussels from the shells and discard the beards.
- Cut the mussels into small cubes and reserve any liquid of mussels.
- Strain the cooking liquid and reserve it.
- In a pan, heat the oil on medium heat and cook the onion till browned, stirring continuously.
- Stir in the celery, potato, carrot and reserved cooking liquid and cook till the vegetables become tender.
- In a large pan, melt the butter and stir in the flour.

- Add the milk and bring to a boil, beating continuously.
- Add the broth and again bring to a boil, beating continuously.
- Remove from the heat and immediately, stir in the vegetable mixture, seasoning and 1/3 of the cooked mussels with their liquid.
- Serve with a topping of the remaining mussels and parsley.

Servings per Recipe: 3

Timing Information:

Preparation	10 mins
Total Time	30 mins

Nutritional Information:

Calories	804.3
Fat	33.3g
Cholesterol	153.3mg
Sodium	1440.9mg
Carbohydrates	70.2g
Protein	54.9g

* Percent Daily Values are based on a 2,000 calorie diet.

EAST COAST MUSSEL CHOWDER

Ingredients

- 2 turkey bacon, chopped (slices of)
- 1 C. onion, chopped
- 3⁄4 C. celery, chopped
- 3⁄4 tsp thyme, chopped
- 2 C. red potatoes, diced
- 2 (8 oz.) bottles clam juice
- 2 C. fresh corn kernels

- 20 mussels, scrubbed and debearded
- 3⁄4 C. half-and-half
- 1⁄2 C. low-fat milk
- 3 tbsp all-purpose flour
- 2 (6 1/2 oz.) cans minced clams, liquid reserved
- 1⁄4 tsp salt
- fresh thyme sprig

Directions:

- Heat a large Dutch oven on medium heat and cook the bacon for about 5 minutes.
- Stir in the celery, onion and chopped thyme and cook for about 8 minutes.
- Add clam juice and potatoes and bring to a boil.
- Reduce the heat to medium-low and simmer, covered for about 9 minutes, stirring occasionally.
- Stir in the mussels and corns and bring to a boil.
- Simmer, covered for about 5 minutes.

- Discard any unopened mussels.
- In a bowl, mix together the milk, half-and-half and flour and beat till well combined.
- Add the clams and flour mixture in the pan and stir to combine.
- Simmer for about 2 minutes.
- Stir in the salt and 2 tbsp of the reserved clams liquid and remove from the heat.
- Serve with a garnishing of thyme sprigs

Servings per Recipe: 6

Timing Information:

Preparation	20 mins
Total Time	40 mins

Nutritional Information:

Calories	329.3
Fat	7.2g
Cholesterol	68.9mg
Sodium	634.3mg
Carbohydrates	39.3g
Protein	27.4g

* Percent Daily Values are based on a 2,000 calorie diet.

Basil Puttanesca Mussels

Ingredients

- 1/2 C. basil
- 1/2 C. Italian parsley
- 1/2 C. walnuts
- 1/4 C. olive oil
- 2 minced garlic cloves
- 2 tbsp lemon juice
- 1/2 tsp salt
- 8 oz. angel hair pasta
- 2 chopped mezzetta sweet red cherry peppers
- 1 chopped tomato
- 1/8 C. sun-dried tomato packed in oil
- 2 tbsp crumbled feta cheese
- 1/8 C. chopped olive, of your choice
- 1 tsp capers
- 3 2/3 oz. smoked mussels
- pepper

Directions

- For pesto in a food processor, add walnuts, fresh herbs, garlic, lemon juice, olive oil and salt and pulse till smooth.
- Prepare the pasta according to package's directions.
- In a large serving dish, place the pesto, pasta and remaining ingredients and toss to coat well.

Servings per Recipe: 4

Timing Information:

Preparation	20 mins
Total Time	20 mins

Nutritional Information:

Calories	471.3
Fat	26.5g
Cholesterol	6.3mg
Sodium	446.2mg
Carbohydrates	49.0g
Protein	11.6g

* Percent Daily Values are based on a 2,000 calorie diet.

JAPANESE MUSSELS

Ingredients

- 2 dozen frozen mussels on the half shell, thawed
- 1 1/2 tbsp half-and-half
- 1 C. japanese mayonnaise, Kewpie brand
- 1 -1 1/2 tsp sriracha sauce
- 1 1/2 tbsp masago smelt roe (small fish eggs)
- instant dashi stock, pellets
- fresh lemon, for garnish

Directions

- Set your oven to broiler.
- Detach the mussels from the shells and again place in the shells.
- In a baking dish, place the mussels.
- In a bowl, add the Hon Dashi pellets and half-and-half and stir till dissolved completely.
- Stir in the mayonnaise and Sriracha till smooth.
- Add the roe and slowly, stir to combine.
- Divide the mixture over each mussel evenly.
- Cook under the broiler for about 15 minutes.
- Serve with a drizzling of the lemon juice.

Servings per Recipe: 6

Timing Information:

Preparation	20 mins
Total Time	35 mins

Nutritional Information:

Calories	4.8
Fat	0.4g
Cholesterol	1.3mg
Sodium	1.5mg
Carbohydrates	0.1g
Protein	0.1g

* Percent Daily Values are based on a 2,000 calorie diet.

PORTUGUESE STYLE MUSSELS

Ingredients

- 2 lbs fresh mussels, scrubbed and bearded
- 1/4 C. olive oil
- 4 garlic cloves, minced
- 2 C. chicken broth
- 1 C. red wine
- fresh parsley, for garnish

Directions

- Discard the mussels that will not close after a light tap.
- In a Dutch oven, heat the oil on medium heat and sauté the garlic for about 5 minutes.
- Add the wine and broth and bring to a boil.
- Add the mussels and simmer, covered for about 2-3 minutes.
- Discard any unopened mussels.
- Serve with a garnishing of the parsley.

Servings per Recipe: 4

Timing Information:

Preparation	5 mins
Total Time	10 mins

Nutritional Information:

Calories	388.0
Fat	19.2g
Cholesterol	63.5mg
Sodium	1033.3mg
Carbohydrates	11.3g
Protein	29.6g

* Percent Daily Values are based on a 2,000 calorie diet.

Spicy Lime Southeast Asian Mussels

Ingredients

- 1 tbsp peanut oil
- 3 medium shallots, thinly sliced
- 2 tbsp sliced peeled fresh ginger
- 4 cloves garlic, smashed
- 1 stalk fresh lemongrass, sliced and smashed
- 1 serrano or Thai bird chili, minced with seeds
- 1/2 C. water
- 2 tbsp Southeast Asian fish sauce
- 1 tbsp light brown sugar
- 4 dozen large mussels, rinsed and beard removed
- 1/4 C. freshly squeezed lime juice, plus wedges for garnish
- 3 tbsp fresh cilantro leaves
- 3 tbsp fresh mint leaves

Directions

- In a large skillet, heat the oil on medium heat and stir fry the shallots, garlic, ginger, chili and lemongrass for about 3 minutes.
- Stir in sugar, fish sauce and water and bring to a gentle simmer.
- Add the mussels and simmer, covered for about 5 minutes.
- Discard any unopened mussels.
- Stir in the mint, cilantro and lime juice.
- Serve with a topping of the lime wedges.

Servings per Recipe: 4

Timing Information:

| Preparation | 15 min |
| Total Time | 8 min |

Nutritional Information:

Calories	285
Fat	9g
Cholesterol	20g
Sodium	30g
Carbohydrates	285
Protein	9g

* Percent Daily Values are based on a 2,000 calorie diet.

AMERICANO PAELLA

Ingredients

- 2 medium ripe tomatoes
- 16 large shrimp, peeled and deveined
- 1 tsp smoked spanish paprika
- fresh ground black pepper
- 1 lb chicken thigh, cut into 1-inch pieces (boneless, skinless)
- 8 oz. Spanish chorizo, cut into 1/4-inch-thick rounds
- 1 -2 tbsp olive oil, as needed
- 1 medium yellow onion, small dice
- 2 medium garlic cloves, finely chopped
- 1 large pinch saffron thread
- kosher salt, to taste
- 4 C. low chicken broth
- 16 mussels
- 2 tbsp coarsely chopped fresh Italian parsley
- 2 medium lemons, cut into 8 wedges each, for serving

Directions

- Set your oven to 350 degrees F before doing anything else and arrange a rack in the middle of the oven.
- Cut the tomatoes in half and remove the seeds.
- Grate the tomato halves in a bowl, leaving the skin. (Pulp and juice should be about 3/4 C.)

- In a bowl, add the shrimp, 1/4 tsp of the paprika, salt and black pepper and toss to coat.
- Refrigerate to marinate before serving.
- In another bowl, add the chicken and sprinkle with the salt and black pepper.
- Heat a paella pan on medium-high heat and cook the sausage for about 2-3 minutes. Transfer the sausage in a bowl.
- In the same pan, add the chicken and stir fry for about 6 minutes.
- Transfer the chicken in a bowl. Reduce the heat to medium and sauté the onion, salt and black pepper for about 5 minutes.
- Stir in the garlic, saffron and remaining paprika and sauté for about 30 seconds. Stir in the tomato pulp with juice and stir fry for about 3 minutes.
- Stir in the rice and increase the heat to medium-high.
- Stir in the broth and place the chicken and chorizo on top.
- Bring to a boil. Reduce the heat and simmer, covered for about 10-12 minutes.
- Remove everything from the heat and insert the marinated shrimp and mussels in the rice mixture.
- Cook everything in the oven for about 10-12 minutes.
- Remove the dish from the oven and keep aside, covered for about 5 minutes before serving.
- Serve hot with a garnishing of lemon wedges and parsley.

Servings per Recipe: 6

Timing Information:

Preparation	15 mins
Total Time	1 hr 45 mins

Nutritional Information:

Calories	592.2
Cholesterol	111.5mg
Sodium	834.8mg
Carbohydrates	61.2g
Protein	33.0g

* Percent Daily Values are based on a 2,000 calorie diet.

Thanks for Reading! Join the Club and Keep on Cooking with 6 More Cookbooks....

http://bit.ly/1TdrStv

To grab the box sets simply follow the link mentioned above, or tap one of book covers.

This will take you to a page where you can simply enter your email address and a PDF version of the box sets will be emailed to you.

Hope you are ready for some serious cooking!

http://bit.ly/1TdrStv

COME ON...
LET'S BE FRIENDS :)

We adore our readers and love connecting with them socially.

Like BookSumo on Facebook and let's get social!

Facebook

And also check out the BookSumo Cooking Blog.

Food Lover Blog

10443798R00070

Printed in Great Britain
by Amazon